Tully Makes Friends

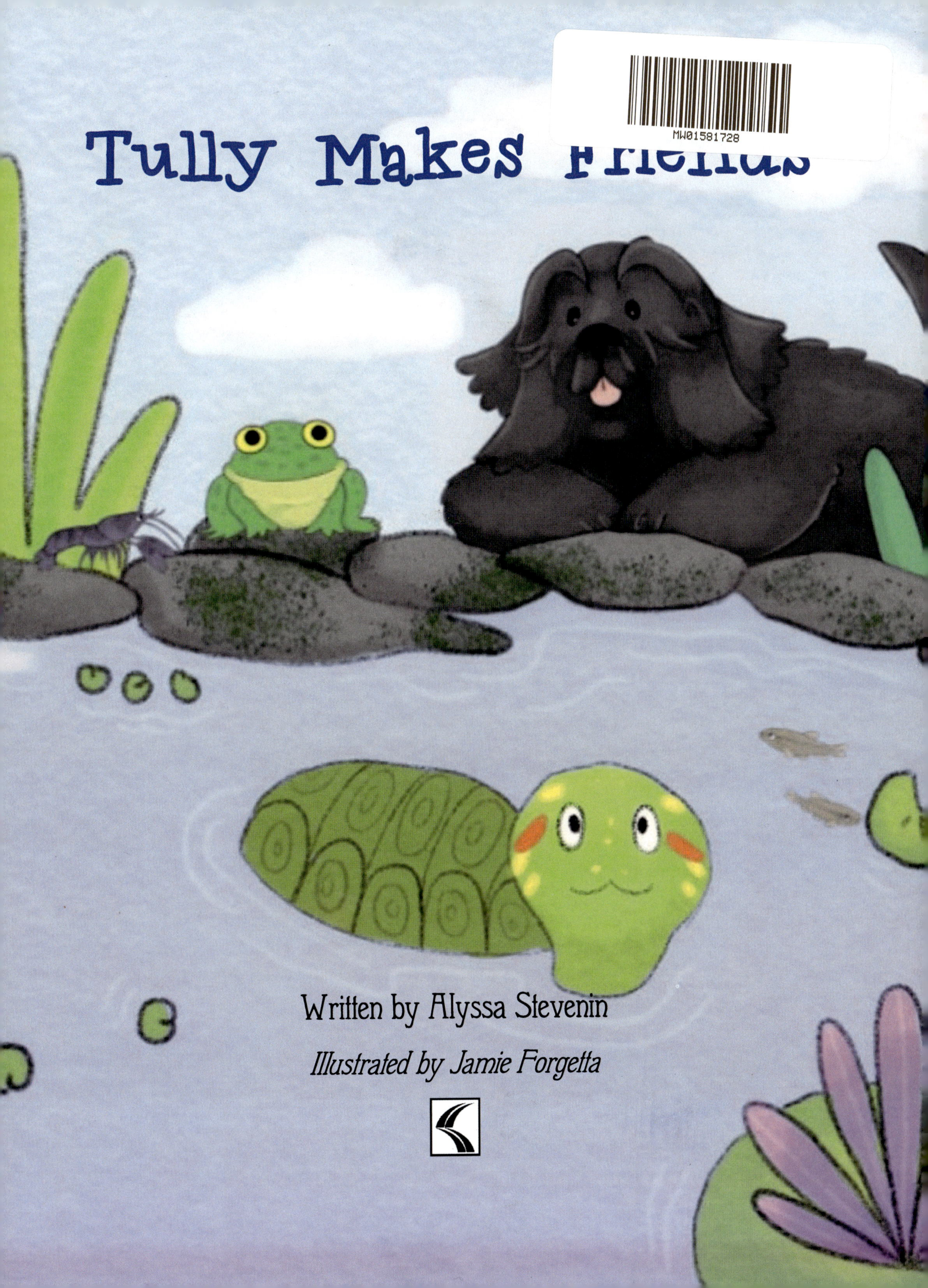

Written by Alyssa Stevenin

Illustrated by Jamie Forgetta

Tully the Turtle
Copyright © 2020 Alyssa Stevenin.

Produced and printed
by Stillwater River Publications.
All rights reserved. Written and produced in the
United States of America. This book may not be reproduced
or sold in any form without the expressed, written
permission of the author and publisher.

Visit our website at
www.StillwaterPress.com
for more information.

First Stillwater River Publications Edition

Library of Congress Control Number: 2020914974

ISBN: 978-1-952521-39-3

1 2 3 4 5 6 7 8 9 10

Written by Alyssa Stevenin
Illustrated by Jamie Forgetta
Published by Stillwater River Publications,
Pawtucket, RI, USA.
Publisher's Cataloging-In-Publication Data
(Prepared by The Donohue Group, Inc.)

Names: Stevenin, Alyssa, author. | Forgetta, Jamie, illustrator.
Title: Tully makes friends / written by Alyssa Stevenin ; illustrated by Jamie Forgetta.
Description: First Stillwater River Publications edition. | Pawtucket, RI, USA : Stillwater River Publications, [2020] | Interest age level: 004-009. | Summary: "Tully is a small, lonely turtle in a big pond. When he is scooped up and brought to an indoor aquarium, he learns to take care of himself and make new friends"--Provided by publisher.
Identifiers: ISBN 9781952521393
Subjects: LCSH: Turtles--Juvenile fiction. | Friendship--Juvenile fiction. | Self-confidence--Juvenile fiction. | CYAC: Turtles--Fiction. | Friendship--Fiction. | Self-confidence--Fiction.
Classification: LCC PZ7.1.S744392 Tu 2020 | DDC [E]--dc23

The views and opinions expressed
in this book are solely those of the author
and do not necessarily reflect the views
and opinions of the publisher.

*This book is dedicated to my children,
and all my students, past and present.*

*I would like to thank Mr. Todd Holden
for his love and support in all our adventures.*

Sitting on the edge of a large pond, Tully the turtle felt very sad and alone. He did not feel so well either. He wasn't good at catching worms like all the other turtles. Tully was also a very small turtle for his age, not big like the other turtles in the pond.

All of a sudden Tully heard something, and then he felt something. Looking down, he could see the pond and all the grass and leaves below. Tully felt like he was floating in the air.

Tully then realized that he was in a net. It was a big green net that just dangled high in the air. His heart felt like it was going to stop. Tully was very frightened.

Tully climbed right into his shell and didn't move at all. He didn't even take a breath. All of a sudden, he felt big hands scoop him up and put him in a dark place. This place was warm. He liked being warm. Rough hands were warming him up. "Are you sick little guy?" Asked the man. Tully thought the man had a kind voice. After a few minutes, Tully felt much better and reluctantly poked his head outside.

The man's hands scooped him up again. Tully thought the man with the kind voice said something, but all of a sudden, he was dropped into warmer water. "I'm rescuing you and taking you to the sanctuary where you will get better," the man said.

After a short amount of time in a big blue pail, Tully was brought to his new home. He was gently placed in a very small pond. *Wow, what is this?* Thought Tully. It had running water, lots of floating plants, and perfectly flat rocks for him to sun himself on. It wasn't too deep, and it wasn't too shallow. It was perfect for him. Tully was very happy here. He swam around all night and sunned himself during the day.

It became easier for him to catch worms. At first the kind man, who someone called Mr. Todd, was giving him mealworms to eat, but then he got better at catching his own. He didn't need Mr. Todd's help anymore. He just needed to practice.

Tully was happy but lonely. Only people and a big shaggy black dog with big eyebrows ever visited the pond. The dog would watch him for hours. The dog never bothered him. He just stared from the edge of the pond.

The next morning, Shaggy barked as a crayfish crawled out from under a log. He seemed to just stay still and not move for hours. Tully began to think this crayfish was cranky.

"I know Shaggy," said the man one day, "he needs a friend." A short time later, the man came back with two small fish. The man said they were called minnows but they both had the same name. Tully was confused. How could they both have the same name? The fish kept to themselves and swam around. They didn't even say "hello" to Tully. Tully started to feel sad all over again. He thought the minnows were mean.

One day, Mr. Todd looked at Tully from the edge of the pond. "How about we go Shaggy," he said to the big black dog. *Go?* Thought Tully, *where are they going? I hope they don't leave me.* Mr. Todd didn't leave for good. He came back, and this time he brought a thing that had beady eyes, a big bump on his back, and smooth skin.

This new thing started talking very fast in a high-pitched squeaky voice. "My name is Squeaky," he said. "I'm a bull frog." He seemed very nice.

Tully poked his head out from inside his shell just a little bit. "I'm Tully," he said. Squeaky turned out to be very funny. He even made the minnows laugh and the crayfish smile. If Tully got stuck in the rocks, or turned upside down in the current, Squeaky pushed him out or flipped him back over.

Squeaky would squeak all night long as he hopped all over the lily pads and cattails. Squeaky would even share a flat rock with Tully on warm days. Tully and Squeaky become best friends. It was so nice to have a best friend, thought Tully. Tully was very happy now. He loved his adventures in the small pond.

The End

About the Author

Alyssa has been a special education teacher for the past 20 years at the preschool level and knows first-hand how to engage children in literacy during early childhood. She reads literacy books in her classroom every day, asks questions of her early learners, and is able to identify what they like and what reaches them. Alyssa has first-hand knowledge of the curriculum and standards needed to effectively teach early learners. She also understands the special needs population at the early literacy level, and knows what accommodations and modifications are needed to reach everyone.

Alyssa is also a mother of three growing boys. Her hobbies include golf, fishing, spending time on the water, and making resin designs. She lives in northern, Rhode Island.

About the Illustrator

"As long as I am doing some form of art I am happy" is how Jamie Forgetta feels in regard to life. A Rhode Island born artist, she discovered her love of drawing at a young age when she would draw her favorite cartoon characters and trace pictures from different kid's books. She graduated from Pratt Institute where she majored in 3D animation, despite this she found a stronger love for the two dimensional form of storytelling. She lives to bring the same joy to others that art brought to her.

Jamie is the author of *The Amazing Monkey Boy*. She has also illustrated more than a dozen books.